GREAT PETS

Guinea Pigs

Ashley Petrylak

Marshall Cavendish
Benchmark
New York

Marshall Cavendish Benchmark
99 White Plains Road
Tarrytown, New York 10591
www.marshallcavendish.us

Library of Congress Cataloging-in-Publication Data

Petrylak, Ashley.
Guinea pigs / by Ashley Petrylak.
p. cm. -- (Great pets)
"Describes the characteristics and behavior of pet guinea pigs, also discussing their physical appearance
and place in history"--Provided by publisher.
Includes bibliographical references and index.
ISBN 978-0-7614-4148-9
1. Guinea pigs--Juvenile literature. I. Title.
SF401.G85.P48 2009
636.935'92--dc22
2008037238

Photo research by Candlepants Incorporated
Front cover: age fotostock / SuperStock
Getty Images: Mike Dunning, 1; Yellow Dog Productions, 4, 12; Paul Bricknell, 7, 19, 29, 31, back cover; Johner
Images, 10; GK Hart/Vikki Hart, 13, 38; Steve Teague, 15, 22, 26, 37; Wendy Ashton, 16; Dorling Kindersly, 18, 20, 32;
Steve Forton and Tim Ridley, 21; Roy Mehta, 28; Malcolm McGregor, 34; Peter Cade, 36; Steve Outram, 40.The Image
Works: Mary Evans Picture Library, 6. Photo Researchers, Inc.: Carolyn A. McKeone, 8, 23, 24.

Editor: Karen Ang
Publisher: Michelle Bisson
Art Director: Anahid Hamparian
Series Design by: Elynn Cohen

Printed in Malaysia
6 5 4 3 2 1

Contents

1

Furry Friends

Have you ever gone to a pet store and seen a group of furry animals running around an open pen? If they were larger than hamsters and smaller than rabbits, then you were probably looking at guinea pigs. Guinea pigs are members of the rodent family and have been kept as pets for more than five hundred years. Today, guinea pigs are one of the most popular pets in the world.

Guinea pigs originally came from the mountains and grasslands of South America where wild guinea pigs still live today. In the wild, guinea pigs live in tall grasses or in burrows. They live in groups of about ten and

Guinea pigs are popular pets that can be found in nearly every pet store across the country.

Around the world, guinea pigs have been kept as pets throughout the years.

help each other gather food and materials for their beds and nests. Because there was little room to raise cattle in the mountainous regions of South America at the time, the natives caught and raised guinea pigs to be used for food. Today, guinea pigs are still raised for food in some areas of South America, though they are also kept as pets.

In the early 1500s, traders from Spain, England, and the Netherlands brought guinea pigs from South America to Europe. These guinea pigs were

Guinea pigs can be wonderful pets, but they are not necessarily right for every home.

domesticated, meaning that people could keep them as pets. Guinea pigs quickly became become popular pets for the upper class. Even Queen Elizabeth I had a guinea pig as a pet! When the British settled in North America, they brought guinea pigs with them to trade and sell. Now, five hundred years later, people still enjoy keeping these good natured animals as pets.

Many people keep guinea pigs because they love to watch their pets run around and play.

When Is a Pig Not a Pig?

No one is exactly sure how the guinea pig got its name. The name may refer to Guiana, a country in South America where guinea pigs live in the wild. Another idea is that the animals may have been sold in Europe for the cost of one guinea coin.

The "pig" part of the name is a little easier to understand. The backside of a guinea pig is similar to the backside of a pig you would find on a farm. But a guinea pig has a short and furry tail instead of a curly tail. Guinea pigs also grunt and squeal just like pigs do. Another name for a guinea pig is a cavy because their scientific name is *Cavia asperea* or *Cavia porcellus*. In Latin, *cavia* means "little" and *porcellus* means "pig."

2

Is a Guinea Pig Right for You?

Guinea pigs make great pets for many families. Most of these furry little creatures are not too hard to care for, and will rarely bite unless they are handled improperly. Guinea pigs are very curious animals. They love to explore their pens or cages and will even hide or run through cardboard tubes or paper cups. Guinea pigs will play during the day and sleep at night. Before you decide to get a guinea pig you should do research on what these small pets are like, what supplies they need, and how to care for them.

An average guinea pig is about 10 to 12 inches long and weighs between 2 and 3 pounds. Guinea pigs have plump bodies and very short legs. Because of their short legs, guinea pigs are not very good at running or

There are many different breeds of guinea pigs to choose from.

Before deciding on any kind of pet, it is a good idea to do a lot of research and visit pet stores to see what might be right for you.

climbing. A guinea pig has a short neck and its head is very close to the ground. In the wild, this makes it easy for it to eat grass or food that is on or near the ground. They are not as large as a cat or a dog, so guinea pigs do not need as much space, but they do need a comfortable cage that is big enough for them to move around.

Guinea pigs have four sharp front teeth and smaller back teeth. Like all rodents, a guinea pig's front teeth never stop growing. To keep their front teeth from growing too long, guinea pigs will chew on sticks or wood blocks to wear the teeth down. Because they are so fond of chewing on things, it is important to keep harmful objects away from your guinea pig. A guinea pig will chew on just about anything it finds. You

Like any pet, guinea pigs have specific needs that you must meet if you keep one as a pet.

will have to provide it with the right toys to chew on in order to keep its teeth in check.

Many new guinea pig owners do not realize that guinea pigs are very noisy animals. Pigs make many different sounds like squeaks, squeals, clucks, whistles, grunts, and purrs. These sounds help a guinea pig communicate with its owner and other pigs. For example, a pig will squeal when it is scared or hurt. When a pig is angry it will chatter its teeth.

Guinea pigs have very good senses, but their sense of smell is their strongest sense. A guinea pig can recognize objects and other guinea pigs by their smell even if they cannot see them. You might observe your guinea pig sniffing the air at times. It is probably trying to see if there are any other pigs nearby. Each guinea pig has a different scent. Often guinea pigs will mark objects with their scent by rubbing their cheeks, back, or tail on the object. This tells other pigs that the object is off limits.

Guinea pigs also communicate their feelings using actions. If you see two guinea pigs rubbing their noses together, they are saying hello to each other. But if you observe a guinea pig open its mouth and show its teeth, be careful! This action means that the pig is angry. Sometimes when a guinea pig is afraid, it will lie very still on its back and pretend to be dead. In the wild, a guinea pig will do this so that the animal that is scaring it will think it is dead and leave.

How Many Pigs are Best for You?

Guinea pigs are very social animals and in the wild usually live with other guinea pigs. If you decide to get more than one guinea pig it is important to make sure that you have enough space and supplies to care for them. You should also think about whether you get two males, two females, or one of

Careful research will help you choose the guinea pig that is perfect for you.

each. Two female pigs will get along better in the same cage than two male pigs. Be careful not to put a male and a female pig in the same cage or else they may breed and you will soon find yourself with a lot of baby guinea pigs running around. No matter how many guinea pigs you decide to get, you have to be sure that you are willing to provide them with supplies, food, and the attention they need.

3

Choosing a Guinea Pig

Today there are more than forty varieties of guinea pigs. Some have short, straight hair, some have long, silky hair, and others have coarse hair that grows in twists and swirls.

Types of Guinea Pigs

Short-haired guinea pigs have a short, glossy **coat.** This is the easiest breed of guinea pig to care for because they do not need to be brushed every day. Peruvian guinea pigs have long silky hair that grows all the way to the ground. Peruvians must be groomed every day and their hair must be brushed away from their eyes.

Abyssinian guinea pigs have short hair that grows in swirls and twists—called whorls—all over their bodies. Waxy Rex guinea pigs have short hair that feels very coarse to the touch.

A guinea pig's coat can be black, brown, red, white, or a combination of these colors. A "self" colored guinea pig has a single color on its coat. A "non-self" colored coat can have up to three colors. Sometimes a guinea pig's coat can have two colors on each hair. This is called an **agouti** coat.

Guinea pigs come in a wide range of colors and fur types, but you might find you like one type better than another. No matter what they look like, guinea pigs make great pets.

Long-haired guinea pigs look really cute, but you have to be ready to do the extra grooming that their coats require.

Where to Get Your Guinea Pig

Once you have decided to get a guinea pig, you will need to figure out where to get it. Pet stores are the most popular places to get a guinea pig. Most stores will have a variety of different guinea pigs of different breeds, colors, and ages. Many people like to get their guinea pigs from pet stores because they can buy the supplies they need at the same time.

Guinea pigs can also sometimes be found at local animal shelters or rescue organizations. These organizations provide homes for different types of animals that have been rescued or whose owners could no longer take care of them. Shelters will occasionally have young guinea pigs as well as adult pigs.

If you are looking for a specific breed of guinea pig, your may have the best luck by going to a guinea pig **breeder**. A guinea pig breeder is

Guinea pigs are very popular because of their size and sweet personalities.

a person who raises certain kinds of guinea pigs. Breeders can be found in newspapers, pet magazines, or online.

Whether you get your guinea pig from a pet stores, shelter, or a breeder, you should be very carful about looking at the guinea pigs. Look at the place where the pigs are kept. Are there a lot of pigs squeezed together in a small cage or tank? Does the cage look clean? If the cage looks dirty with a lot of droppings and mess, it is likely that the guinea pigs are not well cared for. The guinea pig cage should also have fresh food and water. Guinea pigs without proper food and water may be sick and it also means that the guinea pigs are not being properly cared for. You should not get any guinea pigs from a place like that.

Take time to watch the guinea pigs and see how they behave. Are they active? Do they run around and play,

Guinea pigs and rabbits can get along, but you should not get your pig from a pet store that keeps rabbits and guinea pigs together in the same cage.

Trips to the veterinarian are important for keeping your guinea pig healthy, but if you pick out one that is very sick, you may end up going to the vet very often.

Most pet stores do not sell hairless guinea pigs because—though they are cute—they require more work than other types of guinea pigs.

eat, and drink? If they are not sleeping, but look very slow or inactive, they may be sick. Do the guinea pigs get along? They should not be fighting with each other.

Look at their coats—especially if they are long coated. Do the coats look clean and free of dirt and tangles or bare spots? Also look at the pigs' eyes, which should be clear, and feet, which should be clean and free of wounds.

Do not be afraid to ask questions. Ask the pet store worker, shelter worker, or breeder any questions you may have. Ask about how old the guinea pigs are and where they are from. Also be sure to ask how long the pigs have been there. If you are looking at a shelter, ask them why the pig is up for adoption. This is important in case the pig does not like to be held or cannot be with other guinea pigs.

Learning as much as you can about your guinea pig will help you care for your pet.

Trustworthy people who are selling guinea pigs will be happy to answer your questions. If they do not want to answer your questions or cannot provide answers that you are happy with, you should consider going somewhere else.

One of the most important things about choosing a guinea pig is to make sure the two of you get along well together. Take some time to play with and hold your guinea pig to see how it reacts to being around you. If you are getting two pigs, make sure they play well together and do not fight. It is important to be comfortable with your new friend. You want to make sure you bring home a healthy guinea pig that is right for you.

4

Life with Your Guinea Pig

Before you bring home your guinea pig, make sure you have and set up all of its supplies. This will help your guinea pig settle in, and will make it easier for both of you to adjust to each other.

Your Guinea Pig's Home

Your guinea pig needs a safe living area for sleeping and playing. Each guinea pig needs at least 2 square feet of space. If you have more than one guinea pig you will need to make sure you have enough space.

Before you buy or build a home for your guinea pig you need to decide where you will house it. Some families keep their guinea pigs inside the house, while others keep their pigs outdoors. No matter if they are indoors or out, your guinea pig's home should be out of the bright

With the proper supplies, hard work, and patience, you can have a happy and healthy pet guinea pig.

sunshine, kept away from chilly drafts, and should allow you to easily look inside at your pet.

If you decide to keep your guinea pig indoors, you have the option to buy a cage from a pet shop. These cages are often rectangular in shape with thick wire walls and a removable plastic bottom. This type of bottom will make it easy to clean out the cage. Make sure to keep your indoor cage out of the reach of other pets in your home. Cats and dogs are much bigger than your guinea pig and will frighten it if they get too close.

Outdoor cages are sometimes called **hutches** and are usually made of thick, strong wood and wire. Often hutches are used to hold more than one guinea pig. A hutch is usually built on stilts 2 to 3 feet above the ground to

Most people keep their guinea pigs in cages with plastic bottoms that are easy to clean.

prevent chilly drafts from entering. A hutch should also protect your pigs from the rain. You will also be able to see your pets more easily with a raised hutch. Outdoor hutches can be built with two rooms for your pigs. One of the rooms can be used for sleeping and the other can be used for playing and eating. You should be aware, however, that an outdoor hutch may attract neighborhood pets, such as dogs and cats, or wild animals, such as raccoons, that will try to get to your guinea pig.

There are certain things you will need to make your cage or hutch a comfortable home for your guinea pig. You can use newspapers or other soft paper to line the bottom of the cage. Since guinea pigs tend to use the bathroom in the same area as their playground, this will come in handy to absorb some urine. Make sure not to use sawdust or hard wood chips because the dust can cause lung problems in your pig.

For the pig's sleeping area you can pile some shredded newspapers, wood shavings, or hay in a corner of the cage. Pet stores sell special houses and tubes where your guinea pig can sleep. Some people use empty flower pots that have been cleaned. Your guinea pig may also use this area to hide if it senses danger or is afraid.

Your guinea pig will need a heavy ceramic food dish in his cage. Make sure not to buy a plastic dish, since your pig may chew on it and swallow harmful plastic pieces. Most importantly, you should always make sure that your pig has a supply of fresh, clean water. Most pet stores will sell water bottles that only let water out when the animal sucks on a tube on the end of the bottle. The cage or hutch should also have toys your guinea pig can use to chew on. Special guinea pig toys can be found at pet stores.

Feeding Your Guinea Pig

Guinea pigs love to eat. In fact, an adult guinea pig will eat for about six hours out of every day. Guinea pigs are **herbivores**, or animals that eat only

Guinea pigs should be offered a bowl of special dry guinea pig food.

Many guinea pigs enjoy treats like apples.

plants, vegetables, and grasses. Herbivores do not eat any meat. Your guinea pig should always have fresh hay or grass available to eat in its cage. It will also enjoy eating raw and cooked vegetables. Your guinea pig should also be fed special guinea pig pellets that have the correct amount of vitamins and minerals your pig needs. These pellets can be bought at pet stores.

Other dry foods that your pet may enjoy include hay, oats, whole-grain crackers, or shelled nuts. Your pig will also enjoy softer fruits and vegetables with a lot of liquid in them, such as apples, oranges, berries, carrots, celery, or lettuce. When feeding your pet fruits and vegetables, make sure to wash each piece well under running water to remove any dirt or chemicals.

You should feed your guinea pig at the same times every day and should make sure that it always has pellets and hay to eat throughout the day. When feeding your pig, fill the bowl with pellets. Your pig will only eat as much as it needs. In the evening you should feed your pig one slice of fresh fruit or one handful of chopped vegetables. Do not feed your pig wilted or spoiled greens or potato peelings. These foods will make your pig sick.

Your pig should have clean and fresh water from its bottle. Every day you must be sure to wash the pig's water bottle and refill it with clean water. The drinking water should not be too hot or too cold.

Handling Your Guinea Pig

When you pick out your guinea pig, you can ask the store worker or breeder to show you how to hold it. The first couple of times you hold our guinea pig, have an adult help you. To safely pick up your guinea pig you should stroke its back gently and then slip one hand underneath the pig. Place the other hand on the pig's shoulders and lift it up safely and securely. You can keep the guinea pig pressed against you or cupped in your arms to keep it safe.

Always sit on the floor when holding your pig. That way if it jumps out of your arms it will not get hurt from a long fall. Holding your pig often will help it get used to you. But if the pig struggles a lot and squeals a lot, put it down gently and let it calm down.

Like any animal, guinea pigs need to exercise to stay healthy. You can let your guinea pig play in a closed room. However, you need to watch your pig at all times when it is out of the cage so it does not chew on wires or eat objects that could be harmful.

If it is a nice day outside, you may choose to play with your pig outdoors. A fun way to do this is to build a secure outdoor area for your pet filled with interesting objects and activities. Guinea pigs also like to climb up and down ramps. You can easily build a ramp in your play area with flat, smooth pieces of wood and bricks. When your guinea pig is outside, it is likely that it will eat a lot of grass. Before bringing your pig outside, make sure that the grass has not been treated with any harmful chemicals. This could make your guinea pig very sick. Some people use special leashes or harnesses when taking their pig outside. Never let your pig run around outside in an open area or without a leash or harness. Your pig can run away or be hurt.

Keeping Your Guinea Pig Healthy

One of the most important parts of owning a pet is keeping it healthy. Before you bring home your guinea pig, you should find a **veterinarian**

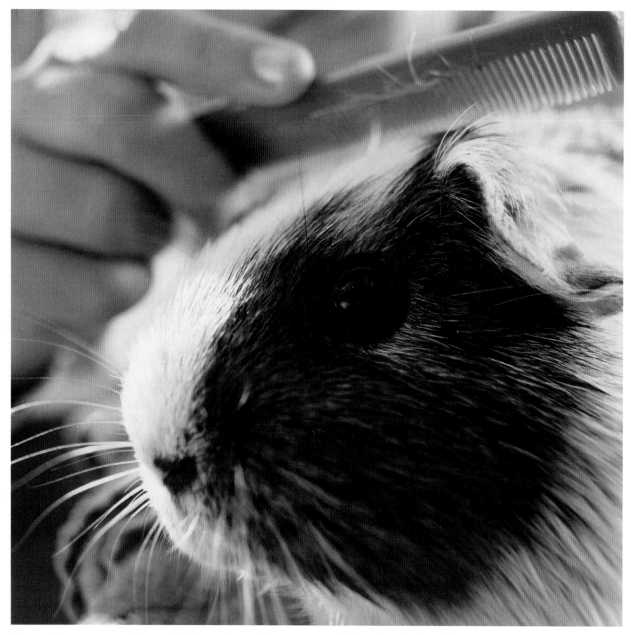

Grooming your guinea pig is an important part of keeping it healthy.

Allowing your guinea pig time to explore and run around is an important part of making sure your pig stays healthy and happy.

who will help you take care of it. A veterinarian, or vet for short, is a special animal doctor. You can find vets in your phone book, in the newspaper, or online. You must make sure that the vet you choose treats small animals like guinea pigs.

After you bring your pet home, you should arrange a visit to your vet. The vet can examine your pig to make sure it is healthy. He or she will weigh the pig, check its heartbeat, and look into its eyes and ears to make sure they are clean and working correctly. The vet will also be able to confirm the gender of the guinea pig. If you have any questions about how to care for your guinea pig, the vet will be able to answer them for you.

One of the best ways to keep your guinea pig healthy is to wash your hands before and after you handle it. Guinea pigs cannot catch diseases from humans, but they can become sick if germs from other animals are on your

Exercise is important for healthy guinea pigs.

hands. The most common cause of sickness in guinea pigs is lack of cleanliness in their environment. Always make sure to remove any soft foods from your pig's cage after a few hours so they do not spoil and attract insects. Also make sure to change you pig's bedding daily. Harmful germs can grow in damp or moist bedding.

Guinea pigs spend a good deal of time grooming themselves so you will not need to bathe your pig often. They will comb their fur with their long teeth and back claws and will wash themselves with their tongues. If you do need to give your pig a bath, you should use a special guinea pig shampoo and wash in a basin filled with a few inches of warm water. After your pig is clean, wrap it in a soft towel and sit it next to a hot water bottle to dry so it does not get cold.

Your guinea pig's fur should be brushed every few days, or every day if you own a long-haired breed. As you brush the fur, check to make sure that your pet's coat is in good condition. A healthy guinea pig's fur should be soft and clean and have no smell.

You should check your guinea pig's eyes and ears every day to make sure they are clean and healthy. You may also want to check to see that its teeth and claws are in good condition. Healthy teeth should be white, short, and straight. Healthy claws should not be too long. Your pig's nails should be trimmed when they get long. Your vet can do this for you or show you how to do it with special nail cutters. If you notice any changes in your pet's teeth or claws, call your veterinarian. If you notice that your pig has a runny nose, watery eyes, or difficulty breathing, you should bring your pig to the vet. If your guinea pig becomes sick, it is important to remove the sick animal from any other animals to prevent germs from spreading.

Guinea pigs are very dedicated animals that will be wonderful companions for you and your family. If you provide your guinea pig with a safe and comfortable place to live, healthy food and clean water, exercise, and regular grooming, your new best friend will remain happy and healthy for many years.

When properly cared for, guinea pigs can provide you with several years of companionship.

Glossary

agouti—A type of guinea pig coat characterized by having two different colors on each individual hair.

breeder—A person who raises certain kinds of guinea pigs.

coat—An animal's fur or hair.

domesticated—Describes an animal that has been bred to live with humans as a pet.

herbivore—An animal that eats only plants. Herbivores do not eat meat.

hutches—A shelter for a small animal such as a guinea pig or rabbit.

gnaw—The act of chewing or biting.

veterinarian—A doctor trained to treat different species of animals.

Find Out More

Books

Bozzo, Linda. *My First Guinea Pig and Other Small Pets.* Berkeley Heights, NJ: Enslow Elementary, 2008.

Loves, June. *Guinea Pigs and Rabbits.* Philadelphia: Chelsea Clubhouse, 2004.

Spengler, Kremena. *Caring for Your Guinea Pigs.* Mankato, MN: Capstone Press, 2008.

Tourville, Amanda Doering. *Scurry and Squeak: Bringing Home a Guinea Pig.* Minneapolis, MN: Picture Window Books, 2008.

Websites

Comfy Cavies
http://www.comfycavies.com/
Created by two guinea pig owners, most of the website is dedicated to teaching new guinea pig owners everything from how to choose their pig to their daily care.

Guinea Pig Care from ASPCA'S ANIMALAND

http://www.aspca.org/site/PageServer?pagename=pets_guineapigcare

The American Society for the Prevention of Cruelty to Animals (ASPCA) sponsors this site for children who want to learn more about caring for a pet guinea pig. The website features games, activity sheets, cartoons, and a lot of information about caring for many different types of pets.

Guinea Pigs Club

http://www.guineapigsclub.com

This site is perfect for people who already own a guinea pig or are interested in getting one. In addition to a lot of helpful information about housing, feeding, and breeding pigs, there are also a lot of fun games and activities.

How to Care for Guinea Pigs

http://www.humanesociety.org/pets/pet_care/rabbit_horse_and_other_pet_care/how_to_care_for_guinea_pigs.html

This website sponsored by the Human Society gives guinea pig owners tips about how to care for their small pets.

Index

Page numbers for illustrations are in **bold**.

About the Author

Ashley Petrylak is a freelance writer and medical publisher living in New York City. She grew up in Philadelphia and spent her summers caring for her classrooms' pets, including guinea pigs, gerbils, and hamsters. She loves all animals, big and small, and has had cats, dogs, and even rats as pets.